The

Year

of the

Poet II

November 2015

The Poetry Posse

inner child press, ltd.

The Poetry Posse 2015

Jamie Bond
Gail Weston Shazor
Albert 'Infinite the Poet' Carrasco
Siddartha Beth Pierce
Janet P. Caldwell
Jackie Allen
Tony Henninger
Joe DaVerbal Minddancer
Neetu Wali
Shareef Abdur – Rasheed
Kimberly Burnham
Ann White
Keith Alan Hamilton
Katherine Wyatt
Fahredin Shehu
Hülya N. Yılmaz
Teresa E. Gallion
William S. Peters, Sr.

General Information

The Year of the Poet II
November Edition

The Poetry Posse

1st Edition : 2015

Publisher Information

1st Edition : Inner Child Press :
intouch@innerchildpress.com
www.innerchildpress.com

ISBN-13 : 978-0692569849 (Inner Child Press, Ltd.)
ISBN-10 : 0692569847

$ 12.99

WHAT WOULD LIFE
BE WITHOUT
A LITTLE
POETRY?

Dedication

This Book is dedicated to
Poetry . . .
its Patrons,
the Spirit of our Everlasting Muse
&
the Power of the Pen.

Poets . . .
sowing seeds in the
Conscious Garden of Life,
that those who have yet to come
may enjoy the Flowers.

Foreword

Poetry is the medium that poets use to gift the world with their offerings, their verse. Without these gifts the world would be less blessed. We, as members of the 2016 Poetry Posse II, have been richly blessed with the gift of poetry that has the power to inspire and brighten the lives of others.

Apart from poems like *Roses are Red, Violets are Blue,* the first poem I remember being introduced to came at the knees of my grandmother. She had recited a poem to me and I was so smitten that I sat down and memorized it. Apparently I was around five or six years old when I copied that poem down, making sure the letters rested on the lines of the paper. And yet, today, I remember neither the poem nor its name.

Excited, I placed *my* poem in an envelope and affixing a postage stamp, I walked down the road to the mailbox which was below my grandparents' home. I raised the little red flag on the mailbox to alert the postman to stop and pick up my poem. I had just entered a poetry contest. Sponsored by the *Saturday Evening Post*, I waited, and waited to hear back from the publisher. I hoped to learn that I had won first place. Alas, that never happened. As far as I know, my poem never appeared in the magazine.

Whenever I look back on that childhood effort, I think that it's possible that my grandmother may just have retrieved "my poem" from the mailbox to prevent me from being accused of plagiarism. It never occurred to me to ask her. Eventually, I forgot about the disappointment, that is, until, in elementary school, I received an assignment to write a poem.

Following a half hour's introduction to poetry, my fourth grade teacher assigned my class to, "Write a poem tonight and be prepared to read it aloud tomorrow." I fussed and fumed. Complaining to my mother, I said, "It isn't fair. After one lesson I'm supposed to write a masterpiece and read it before the class? If I had but one lesson in violin, would I then be required to play a piece of music the next day, and in front of the class?"

Finally, I wrote something in the form of that simplistic poem, *Roses are Red, Violets are Blue.* Needless to say, I was disappointed with what I'd written, feeling like I had cheated because my poem was not original and sounded too much like *Roses are Red, Violets are Blue.* Angry with my teacher for placing me in such a humiliating position, I was also angry at myself because I had wanted to write something profound.

Giving up is not an option for one who has the fire, the passion that longs to be expressed. At first opportunity, and as a young housewife, I began to express my creative voice by painting on canvases. Much later, and with maturing confidence, I discovered that I could also express my voice by writing, the old self accusations having passed away.

I can only imagine what my fourth grade teacher might say, were I able to hand her a copy of my first book published this year, *Looking for Rainbows, Poetry, Prose and Art.* I dare say, she'd be proud of me.

Perhaps, you will also choose to make a list, as I have done, and lift up with thanks and gratitude all who have encouraged, inspired, and supported, you, even adding to the list those situations that may have led to your becoming the poet you are today.

I Am Thankful...

... that I had a grandmother, whose serendipitous recitation of a poem, instilled in me the love of poetry.

...that I have been given the gift of loving all things related to poetry, the study and sound of the words as they leave my mind and appear on the page, and for fingers that type quickly enough to keep up with my ideas and thoughts.

...for teachers who subtracted points from my papers for omitting punctuation marks, for failing to dot the i's and for neglecting to cross the t's."

... that I am am not anxious about revealing myself through my writings. And, where ever did that come from?

... that I signed up for a writing class, and although I contemplated many reasons, many excuses as to why I should not open the door and take my seat, I am thankful that I rejected that fear.

...for the poetic drive that disciplines me to keep on studying, learning and sharing my work,

...for my poetic path even though it took me decades to discover my way and that I found places where I was able to share my poetry, for example: Facebook, Inner Child, The Voices, The Candle, Generation 21 and PoemHunter.

... for my husband, family, old and new friends, for classmates who follow my poetry, for William S. Peters, Sr., and for other poets who believed in me and encouraged me and who still do.

For these, my mother's words, I owe a debt of gratitude:

"As long as there's breath, there's life. And, as long as there's life, there's time to begin that which you've always wanted to do. So, begin."

Jackie Davis Allen
2015 November 1

Preface

Dear Family and Friends,

As we come to the close of the year of 2015, i would like to express my gratefulness for every member of The Poetry Posse. We are one month away from concluding our second year in this effort, *The Year of the Poet*. Over the past 23 months, we have featured many Poets from our Global Poetry Family, and shared them with you. We are looking forward to continue in this process of the offering of our Verse.

You may or may not be aware that the cost of this effort is fully underwritten by Inner Child Press. (www.innerchildpress.com). On another important note, we are also currently in the process of taking in submissions for the World Healing, World Peace Anthology. This project has been active since 2011, and the upcoming 2016 publication will be our 3rd installment where Poets from all over the world contribute their voices pertaining their thoughts, feelings and insights. The Anthology will be published in April of 2016 to coordinate with what we call **International Poetry Month**.

Words are powerful instruments that have a greater potential for change than many other efforts we may mobilize. The general consensus amongst most people i speak to these current days all voice a concern and a need for change in how we as humans integrate with each other. There are many challenges within the fabric of humanity that upset the balance and affront the potential of what life can possibly be. Learning to coexist seems at times to be a daunting task. I am so honored to be amongst such wonderful poetic souls who contribute their thoughtful words to that end . . . World Healing, World Peace.

Thank you all for the love.

Bless Up

Bill

Thank God for Poetry
otherwise
we would have a problem !

~ wsp

Table of Contents

The Poetry Posse

Table of Contents . . . *continued*

November Features   111

Poets, Writers . . . know that we are the enchanting magicians that nourishes the seeds of dreams and thoughts . . . it is our words that entice the hearts and minds of others to believe there is something grand about the possibilities that life has to offer and our words tease it forth into action . . . for you are the Poet, the Writer to whom the Gift of Words has been entrusted . . .

~ wsp

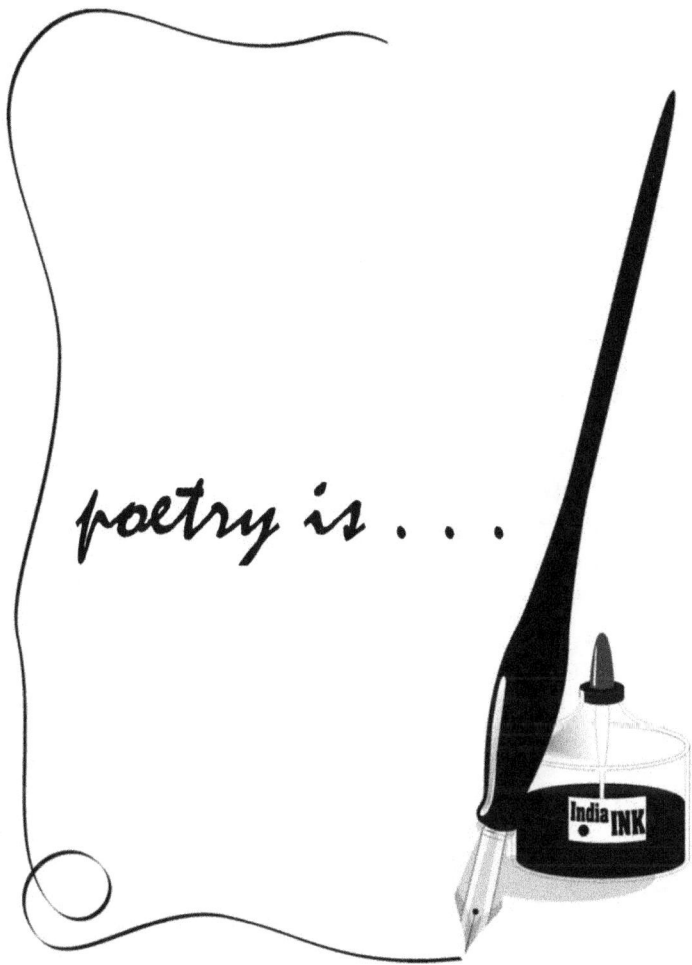

poetry is . . . .

The
Year
of the
Poet II

November 2015

The Poetry Posse

inner child press, ltd.

Poetry succeeds where instruction fails.

~ wsp

Gail
Weston
Shazor

This is a creative promise ~ my pen will speak to and for the world. Enamored with letters and respectful of their power, I have been writing for most of my life. A mother, daughter, sister and grandmother I give what I have been given, greatfilledly.

Author of . . .
"An Overstanding of an Imperfect Love"
&
Notes from the Blue Roof
available at Inner Child Press.

www.facebook.com/gailwestonshazor
www.innerchildpress.com/gail-weston-shazor
navypoet1@gmail.com

Seven times Seven

I dreamed of sevens last night.
Slight and subtle sevens floating
In the air above our bed
I counted them as they appeared
Seven times seven brushes of teeth
Seven passes of my hair brush
Seven steps between my shoes and and yours
You rested under a quilt of seven colors
Gently and quietly snoring
I could only smile in my dream you
Your smile breaks the beauty of your face
You say in seven syllables
Happy Anniversary
I kiss you seven times in response
And slip back under our seven colored quilt for hugs
In this quiet solitude we are still
Awaiting the seven AM alarm
You rise and I descend seven steps
To make the coffee
Where I find a young man
At the table counting to himself
He smiles up at me and
I brush the hair back from his forehead
He tells me that he has memories his time tables
All the way through seven.
In this season
We are in completion.

Upcoming

Pan tribal
Span Afreeka
My arms outreached
Circle the earth
Limbs ease in mahogany
And the red clay goddess
Creates a primal yearning
In many hues
A high yellow sun
Kisses my brow
Across Sahara Sands
I sometimes dance in the moon
With the abandon of something wild
This is the season of Thanksgiving
And I pick through the passing days
For something warm to hold onto
My memories of the tribal hut
Will have to hold me through
The coming winter

Winter

Light aggressively
Forces rain and wind to flee
It's time is up

The wind bellows hard
From the onset of Ares
It's how things change

"Let slip" it is said
And the stars begin to move
Lightning splits the sky

Moon changes orbits
The days begin to shorten
Winter is now here.

Albert
'Infinite the Poet' Carrasco

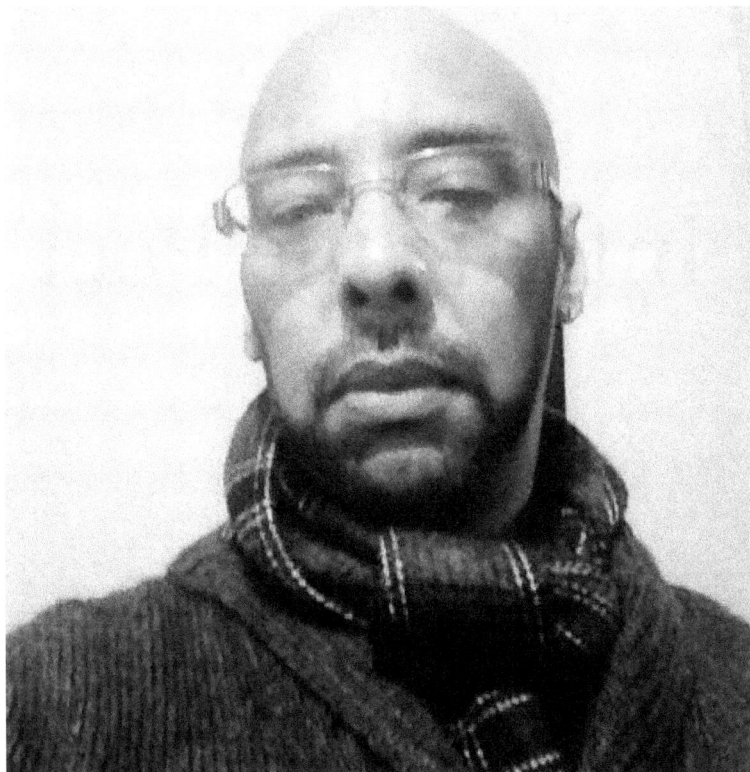

I'm a project life philanthropist, I speak about the non ethical treatment of poor ghetto people. Why? My family was their equal, my great grandmother and great grandfather was poor, my grandmother and grandfather, my mother and father, poverty to my family was a sequel, a traditional Inheritance of the subliminal. I paid attention to the decades of regression, i tried to make change, but when I came to the fork in the road and looked at the signs that read wrong < > right, I chose the left, the wrong direction, because of street life interactions a lot around me met death or incarceration. I failed myself and others. I regret my decisions, I can't reincarnate dead men, but I can give written visions in laymens. I'm back at that fork in the road, instead of it saying wrong or right, I changed it, now it says dead men < > life.

Infinite poetry @lulu.com
Alcarrasco2 on YouTube
Infinite the poet on reverbnation

Infinite Poetry

http://www.lulu.com/us/en/shop/al-infinite-carrasco/infinite-poetry/paperback/product-21040240.html

Changed

I'm not in debt to anyone but my children, to them I owe my life, my time, my everything. When i think of them, those beautiful visions keep me from falling victim and calling connections. Dudes see me and say al you've changed, I say I evolved, couldn't be stagnated while six sextillion pounds of rock and 3/4 of water revolves, I've gained momentum, I'm now the eyes for those that can't see, my written is for the hard of hearing, I'm the brains for those ignorant to education living in mental armageddon.

I know the feeling of being poor, I know the feeling of being rich, I now how it feels to have holes in your body that can't get stitched, I know how it is to see your homies six feet below and instead of throwing in flowers I wanted to throw myself in that ditch...ain't that a bitch! I know the ghetto Geneva convention, that's war in the streets, and that's never leave your house without your vest and gun, never trust anyone, trusting the wrong ones can get you a white sheet while you bleed out in the slums, I've seen it happen to many suns...Solstices in eternal eclipses. I got the power to uplift these fallen stars with poetic bars, I know the life of rectangle bars, jail bars, The life of being imprisoned with no bars, that's why daily I share my mental scars. I've changed

The underdog

I learnt everything in life through trial and era, the odds would be stacked up against me, I would still try to climb over, I taught myself to understand that failure was the first steps to success, so I failed over and over until I mastered movements, life to me was like chess. Through every loss and defeat I gained experience, knowledge, education, That's why on my final lap In situations i remembered how I was trapped, knew how to react, made quick decision to make precise evasions... loosing so much I became a veteran. I'm a goal chaser like the reaper is the soul chaser... I will not give up. Anything I target I pursue till I have a lock on it as if I'm chasing a Charlie after taking off from a carrier by the navy as a fighter pilot. I was told I will always be poor, so I tried not to be, they said I would die, so I roamed no mans land cautiously, people told me I would never amount to nothing, those same people now show courtesy due to false assumptions and pre-judging me. Don't let people cover your ideas, thoughts or motivation with an invisible gray cloud, follow your dreams, no matter how long it takes to get there, because when you do emerge from the shroud after being told you'll never do so by haters and naysayers, you'll feel extra proud..

Thanksgiving

This is the month where family and friends from all over get together and sit at the table and enjoy a feast of our culture with one another.

Turkey is stuffed and being baked, white rice, yellow rice with peas, potato salad, macaroni salad, avocado, cranberry sauce and all sorts of pies and cakes.

The traditional Spanish seasoning aroma fills every part of the house... Adobo, sazon, sofrito y recaito and other herbs and spices hand delivered straight from Puerto Rico.

The foundation is handing out secret recipes, you see great grandmothers in the kitchen with their daughter and their daughters daughter getting taught cooking lessons.

A few generations of men are in the living room buzzed on coquito banging on bongos thinking they're el gran combo.

They ladies holler.. dinner is ready! Everybody runs to the table and a prayer is said before the food is fed.

Janet
Perkins
Caldwell

.

Janet P. Caldwell has been writing for 40 years and has been published in print newspapers and held a byline in a small newspaper in TX. She also has contributed to magazines and books globally. She has published 3 books, *5 degrees to separation* 2003, *Passages* 2012, and her latest book *Dancing Toward the Light . . . the journey continues 2013,* and contributed to countless anthologies yearly. She is currently editing her 4th book, written and to be published 2015. All of her Books are available through Inner Child Press, along with Fine Book Stores Globally.

Janet P. Caldwell is also the Chief Operating Officer of Inner Child, which includes the many Inner Child Facebook groups, Inner Child Newspaper, Inner Child Magazine, Inner Child Radio and The Inner Child Press Publishing Company.

To find out more about Janet, you may visit her web-site, Face-book Fan Page and her Author page at Inner Child Press.

www.janetcaldwell.com
https://www.facebook.com/JanetPCaldwell
http://www.innerchildpress.com/janet-p-caldwell.php

Grateful and Pleased

I have lived a good life
been loved by many
have 2 great children
and 4 grandchildren.

I have you, a song in my heart
and more than plenty.
There is nothing that I need and for that
I am eternally grateful, so pleased.

Dreaming of You

A few nights ago
I dreamed of you.
There you were, fair hair
and the smile that melted my heart.

We were young and beautiful
dancing on 6th street in Austin. Some people
stared, we cherished that moment
that we both knew
in a conventional way would not last.

I relived the day that we left work for lunch
and went to your sister's house
making love in that cold room in summer's heat
and forgot the time.

It was *those moments, that now*
that we have taken along life's path.
The moments of gratitude glimmering
in our eyes, when no-one is looking
you wink at me, after all of this time.

Thank you for the love, the romance and fun.
I'll always love you
and one day we'll do it again.
'Til next time, I'll be here
because no-one compares to you.

For the Lady who Ironed my Shirt

You sat quietly on your appointed throne
fussing over your guests
to make all of us feel at home.

Little did you know
what a treat this was for me
as I do my own ironing
washing and cleaning.

I was treated as a Queen
from beginning to end.

When I think of you
it brings a tear to my eye
my sister, my friend.

As I approached you
crumpled shirt in hand
the ironing board seemed
to appear out of nowhere.
You arose as if to set my worries free
I smiled, extended my hand
and your soft eyes gazed at me.

We had a language barrier
but not for long . . .
who could not read
the needs between sisters
and the task set before you
was immediately understood.

Within minutes, there was a gentle
rap on my door. Your smiling face appeared
with my crease-less shirt
on a hanger, dangling from your arm.

I thank you and thanked you
and in your own way
you said that none was needed
it was your pleasure to help me
to begin fresh, to start my day.

Again, When I think of you
it brings a tear to my eye
my sister, my friend.
I love you and your giving ways.

~ ~ ~

Author's Note: More here,
http://www.janetcaldwell.com/for-the-lady-who-ironed-my-shirt/

Jackie
Allen

My name is Jacqueline D. Allen, otherwise known as Jackie. I grew up in the Cumberland Mountains of Appalachia, one of ten children. As a child, of a coal miner and a stay at home mother, I told stories at night to my younger siblings in an attempt to lull them to sleep. That was the tool I used so that I might return to my homework, uninterrupted. Much to my delight they begged me to bring the "books" home so that they could see the pictures for themselves. As delighted as I was that they loved my stories, it was difficult to endure the disappointment on their faces when I told them the truth: I had made up all of the stories that they had so loved.

Many years after those early seeds of story telling began, after college, after work, after raising my children, I began to write poetry. I find writing poetry the creative fabric from which I am able to weave whole cloth from both truth and fiction. Inspired by real life events, memory, imagination and enhanced by the sheer joy of playing with words, my poetry satisfies my need to be creative.

And, if ever there are days when I wonder why it took so long for the writer in me to reveal itself, I simply pick up my pen, or in most cases, go to the computer, and begin writing yet another poem.

This Morning

This morning I awakened
 To skies gray and wet, and as
From the high heavens above
 Streamed down, torrents of intent.

From my window seat, I spied
 A small squirrel, dark and dank,
He was shivering and chattering.
 Then, suddenly, he wisely scattered.

A bolt of destructive bright light
 Startlingly burst into fury's flames.
The clouds, revealing copious tears
 Released their pain, their angst.

No matter name of the season,
 No matter time of day or of night,
Nature delights in revealing different
 And surprising aspects of her face.

Once hidden from my view, I now
 Welcome anew, the face of the sun
Bestowing ardent kisses in colors
 Passionately, bravely bright against blue.

Crossing high over the morning sky
 I receive a gift, a needed reminder;.
It is a rainbow, it is God's promise,
 His covenant graciously renewed.

The Table is Set

Some loosened tongues stained the table
despite the occasion
scattered
upon the presentation
were broken pauses,
shards of glass...
all so boldly released.

Some paradox of relationships reigned
along with sorrow's pain
some came
with woe's tokens
waging gossip,
despairing
blessings
bereft of gratitude.

Some coveted, never introspection,
only greed's wealth
wherever they gathered
with bags of silver
or bags of gold
the bright spotlight
shone solely
upon themselves.

Some strains of self-same songs presumed
inflated images most superior.
sans sensé
of pride,
some poured on salt
and opened old
wounds; some smugly
sang similarly.

Some, praying to God, they desired ,
they dared to make things right
several humbly
sang homilies of gratitude
of love, of forgiveness
and granting reprieves
dispensed gifts
and issued invitations.

Strangely mute, some
neither hungered nor thirsted for truth
yet, kneeling, ashamed
some others begged pardon
for pride of attitude
for misdeeds
for slander.
against others.

A Piece of Heaven

The fog paints a surrealistic scene of the reality of this morning, only the trees nearest my window are visible, their leaves polished a glistening wet. They are silhouetted ghostly against the invisible lane called Hanging Rock.

Like an apparition in a deserted cemetery, the wind, hesitantly accepts the invitation and dances lightly on the leaves swaying, a rocking tempo as if to celebrate the music I hear in the mystical, mysterious, wooded background.

Mother Nature has wrapped the day in a cocoon and blanketed it with caution until its golden orb can release its warmth; and only then, shall I venture out from the little niche where my home rests in heaven's bosom.

Now, fog has lifted her eyes from beneath the curtained veil, and I \wander out onto Crawford's Edge and meander onto the trail of Shamokin Springs, where, descending down below, I meet autumn dancing to a different tune.

Note:
The proper names are those associated with locations within the Blue Ridge Mountains.

Tony
Henninger

Tony Henninger is the current president of The Permian Basin Poetry Society of Texas in West-Texas. His first book, "A Journey of Love", is a collection of love poems dedicated to his wife Deanne and is available at InnerchildPress.Com and Amazon.com.

He has been published in several anthologies including: Permian basin and Beyond 2014, We are the 500 (West Texas poets), Hot Summer Nights 2013 and 2014 editions, and World Healing/World Peace. He is, also, one of the co-authors of the 12 volume Anthology "Year of the Poet 2014" at InnerChild.

He is currently working on his second book of poetry to be published in early 2015.

Born in Frankfurt, Germany and growing up in Colorado, He now resides in Texas.

Tony Henninger on Facebook

Tony Henninger at Linkedin.com

Tony Henninger at Permian Basin Poetry Society @gmail.com.

A SOLITARY MOMENT

Tired though I am, I must keep on swimming
out into the ocean of love and compassion.
Once in that ocean, there is no return.

My soul is on fire, let it burn.

Different dreams at night,
Different paths by day.
I won't get lost in the darkness,
I won't just fade away.

The sadness I see,
oh how many tears,
overwhelming me.
All my years
Spent in giving of my love
like a waterfall.
each sparkling drop
a piece of my soul.

Shadows darken my light
a little more each day.
Watching the world's beauty
silently fall away.

Feeling so alone
in a blinded crowd.
Wanting to cry,
to scream out loud.

Everyone is searching
for a place to belong.
A soulmate perhaps, or
just a place to call home.
Lord, you are my shelter
holding me in and keeping me warm.
As my tears burn my eyes, I realize,
I just want to come home.

In this solitary moment,
I close my eyes
and bleed this empty heart
of all that wants to die,
and drown in your light.

Opening my eyes I see
all of your beauty and how
the world was meant to be.

RECONCILIATION

Just a little more medication
to take the sting out of the pain.
I can barely open my eyes
to try and see through the rain.
You threw me a curve,
letting me think all was ok.
Now, I find myself in this bed
slowly fading away.
You could have shown me
my time was short.
You could have told me
my dreams to abort.
So you leave me with
feelings of loss and regret
for the things I won't experience
and all the beauty I haven't seen yet.
No hint of what is to come,
only pieces gathered on the way.
Fragments you left behind in
this vessel of utter decay.
Should I trust in faith?
Or should I deny it all?
In these last moments
I can hear angels call.
So, ok, take me as you will.
I realize, whether alive or dead,
you will be with me still.
Now, I will put away the feelings
of loss and regret I had before.
I have made my amends
and am yours forevermore.

ESCAPE

How your loveliness fills my night.
Oh, how I dread the coming dawn.
All I need is your sensual love
and then to die in your arms.

Each night I want to wake
to find the starlight in your eyes.
To lose ourselves in rapture
as to the skies we rise.

Moving in desperate rhythm,
oblivious to time and reality,
our fire raging like an inferno,
leaving this universe's duality.

Escaping into the void of space.
Creating another universe,
another reality, where
only passion exists.

Tony Henninger

Joe
DaVerbal
MindDancer

Joseph L Paire' aka Joe DaVerbal Minddancer . . .
is a quiet man, born in a time where civil liberties
were a walk on thin ice. He's been a victim of his
own shyness often sidelined in his own quest for
love. He became the observer, charting life's path.
Taking note of the why, people do what they do.
His writings oft times strike a cord with the
dormant strings of the reader. His pen the rosined
bow drawn across the mind. He comes full-frontal
or in the subtlest way, always expressing in a way
that stimulate the senses.

https://www.facebook.com/joe.minddancer

THANK YOU FOR THAT

Breakfast in bed was very nice this morning
I wasn't expecting such a feast
It's the middle of the week I'm in the middle of yawning
Thank you for that you're so sweet

I found a perfect spot where I can rest tonight
That last beating has left me weary
Life in a shelter may seem a welcome comfort
The cold of the streets has a warmer heart
Thank you for this alley behind a grocery store
I've eating more than I ever have before
The manager knows I sleep there
I believe it's because he's been there
I thank him for that

Hey! I remember you it's been what, 20 years?
After all this time I often wondered about you
I came to you with a story while shedding my tears
You told me it was your last, but gave it without fear
I still don't have that five bucks, what I have is a family
I went to banks, churches, and friends I came up thin
What I got came from a total stranger and not a friend
It was a life changing moment
I still don't have that five bucks
What I had was a bit of luck and a wonderful opportunity
And a continued search of where you might be
So here, take this in gratitude please don't refuse
I have my family now thanks to you

Just that small gesture of kindness
Reminds us being grateful comes back to you.

IT IS A GIFT

There comes a moment when we understand our purpose
When realize our poetry is more than just verse
A women contemplating suicide
Read a poem and decided not to die
The words had nothing to do with her
But somehow the meaning got through to her
In an unrelated incident across town
A man on the verge of divorcing his lady fair
Came across a poem somewhere
From the moment he read it
He was happy he wedded
He proposed to her again right there
From lost souls and broken hearts
To the nervous about making a new start
The words are there
Simple expressions become life lessons
And oh, they can so relate
What we create can be described as a gift
Most are thankful for it
Some don't give a kitty and their words are
Well we'll let's just say less gritty
The gift the blessing or just a way with words
I'll end this by saying I'm thankful for it.

A FLOWER FOR HER HAIR

I picked a Sonja Rose to bring joy for a moment
A Lilly would do in its place or the familiar carnation
When you know her favorite it brings a different elation
Appreciation of her beauty in the form of nature
Could only be a comparison to its texture and soft fragrance
She's not a flower though nor ever green
You can have your perennials
You can have your annuals
She's my bonsai and I've yet to utter the words
I love you
I trim her branches and let grow her stems
She presents me her best leaves
I let her breathe
You can't hold the perfect rose in one place
I give her angles to catch the sun
Tomorrow she'll catch another one
I picked a Sonja Rose today
I placed it in her hair this is not just for you my dear
It's appreciation for women everywhere.

Shareef Abdur Rasheed

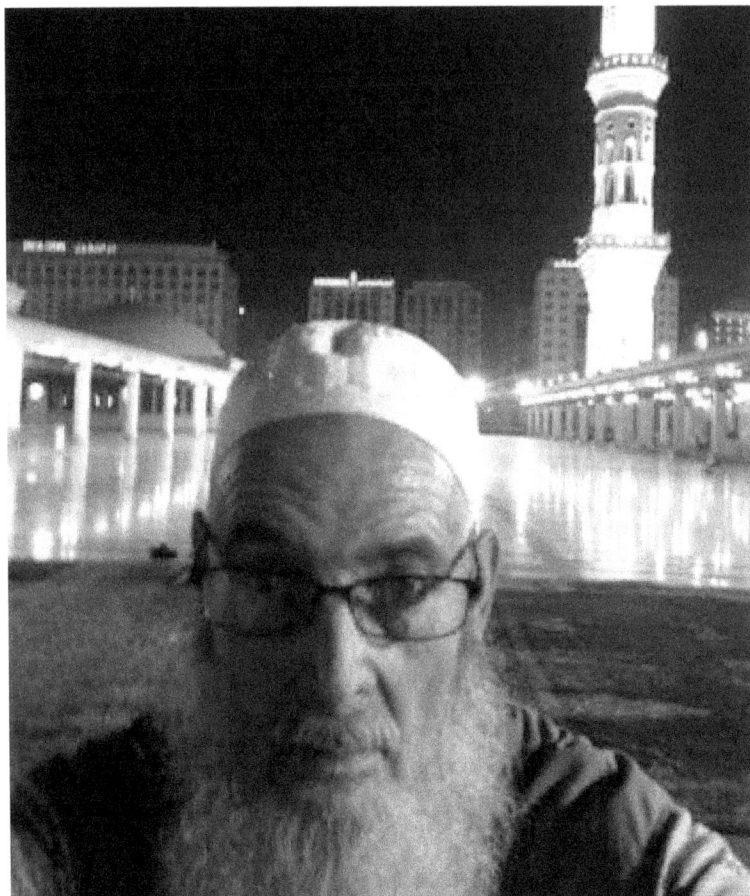

Shareef Abdur-Rasheed, AKA, Zakir Flo was born and raised in Brooklyn, New York. His education includes Brooklyn College, Suffolk County Community College and Makkah, Saudi Arabia. He is a Veteran of the Viet Nam era, where in 1969 he reverted to his now reverently embraced Islamic Faith. He is very active in the Islamic community and beyond with his teachings, activism and his humanity.

Shareef's spiritual expression comes through the persona of "Zakir Flo". Zakir is Arabic for "To remind". Never silent, Shareef Abdur-Rasheed is always dropping science, love, consciousness and signs of the time in rhyme.

Shareef is the Patriarch of the Abdur-Rasheed Family with 9 Children (6 Sons and 3 Daughters) and 42 Grandchildren (24 Boys and 18 Girls).

For more information about Shareef,
contact or follow him at :

http://www.facebook.com/shareef.abdurrasheed1
http://zakirflo.wordpress.com/
http://www.innerchildpress.com/shareef-abdur-rasheed.php
https://www.facebook.com/pages/Muslim-Writers-
Forum/370511683056503

relative to..,

what?
what you got or not
where you've been
what you've seen
done without
strong, patient through out?
what you feel
when suffering of others
reaffirm being real
no home, no clothes, no meal
relative to what?
what you got or not
you complain about what
you don't got
while millions would blow up
your spot
because you got what they
have not
not including attitude
you may not be starving, homeless,
surviving day to day
yet no gratitude
as though your owed
never consider mercy bestowed
just to have food, shelter, clothes
don't miss the water flow
till the water in the well ain't no mo
have you prepared for death while
there's life?
sickness while there's health?
poverty while there's wealth?

be grateful, don't trip
remember life flips
relative to what?
there's always plenty to be thankful
while others don't got
and you wonder why
a word from the wise..,
" there but for the grace of God goes i "

food4thought= education!

sand..,

in the hourglass
observe how fast
the sand past
sifting down
how much longer
before no more is found?
how much longer are we
to be around
on the earth not yet in the
ground
do we give thanks for each
second bestowed
or do we act as though another
is owed?
take time out to think about
all the blessings undeserved
yet extended
before the hourglass empties
and life's ended
how can we complain when
bounties fall like rain?
just because we experience pain
in the course of living
never refrain from gratitude giving
never to delay giving thanks for
every second, minute, hour
divine is the bestower of life, love
to him goes all the glory, power
fact you must know
perpetual gratitude is owed!
savor the flavor of undeserved
merciful favor
while there's still time, neighbor

They say..,

naturalism,quantum physics
every means to avoid the
self inflicted void of soul
made from a dispised fluid
that's referred to as scum
and used in a context of low,
even disgust as in disgusting
and man,ungratefull man
stands,stands out as an open
adversary to who fashioned
his very being from nothing
drop of fluid fertilizing egg
congealed clot,lump of flesh
yes you, me, who is,was, will be
stands out as an open adversary
against the very existence of him
who created,yes you heard me
created all things from nothing
saying " Be " and it was and shall
Be!
to blind spiritually to see
naturalism,quantum physics had
to be designed
it didn't just materialize and say
suprise
i'm here from no where made by
no one
and here's the real trick
creation on all levels absolutely
perfect
by accident

they say..,
" i mean you you really think it's
heaven sent from a realm unseen? "
indeed as is breath,life,death,
gravity,electricity,trimesters of
human development
taste,smell,hearing,sight
yes and you continue to fight
what a useless plight
falsehood vs truth!
darkness vs light!

food4thought!= education!

Kimberly Burnham

As a 28 year-old photojournalist, Kimberly Burnham appreciated beauty. Then an ophthalmologist diagnosed her with a genetic condition, "Consider life if you become blind." From those devastating words, she forged a healing path with insight and vision. Today, a brain health expert, Kimberly helps people experience richer, more nourishing environments.

"People, who feel better, make better choices for themselves, their community and our world."

Her PhD in Integrative Medicine and extensive training in Craniosacral Therapy, Reiki, Acupressure, Integrative Manual Therapy, Health Coaching, and Matrix Energetics enable her to serve as a catalyst, gently shifting your ability to feel better physically, think more clearly, and be more creative.

A 2014 Poetry Posse member, Kimberly and Creating Calm Network's Ann White, assist small enterprises in crafting business booming words and robust social media platforms. Kimberly won SageUSA's 2013 story contest with a poem from *The Journey Home*, chronicling her 3,000 mile Hazon Cross-USA bicycle trip. Her poetry books include, *Live Like Someone Left The Gate Open* and the upcoming *Healing Words—Poetry for Thriving Brains*. With Elizabeth Goldstein she edited the anthology, *Music— Carrier of Intention in 49 Jewish Prayers*.

Experience greater health & success @ (860)221-8510
http://ParkinsonsAlternatives.CreatingCalmNetwork.com
https://www.LinkedIn.com/today/author/39038923
Vision Story: http://youtu.be/JhG3-qwkvVk

Grateful For The Day

Part of asking
forgiveness is sensitivity
really feeling sorrow

Regretful heart stirring
quiet space between
slow breaths
sighs in truth

I feel the pain
shoulders slump
knowing I
should have done better

Grateful for another day
a full life
in which to love
again

The Four Worlds of Gratitude

Emanation
wisdom energy flows
a red heart
still
pondering deep questions
inspired by angels

Creation
relaxing into the blue sky
grappling
flying
like an eagle spreading
gratitude spirals upward

Formation
harmonizing green and blue
earth enveloping
guarding peace like a mother
lioness fired with sensation
thankful for life
shaped emotions

Action
birthing gratitude
leadership building
coaching, lending a hand
strong as a bull
roaming the golden earth

Layers of thankfulness
eagles calling to the bull
wide green pastures
full of life
angels whispering clues

Understand
the strength of a lion
leading and running
into the wind
seeing good all around

Gratitude energy
gracefully
weaving nature
into an open heart

Body and mind
breathing in soul
spirit carving outward
nature's appreciation

Dance of Hope

And to war
we say
not in my house
remembering
always remembering
we are the mothers
of this earth
home to all of us

Grateful for a moment of hope
in a whirl of colors
red scarves, sunny shirts,
turquoise pants
so much diversity

Sheroes dancing
women of every religions
creeds whirling
as we breathe the same air
feel our bodies
spirit amplifying
love

Returned
recommitting to a world of peace
flags wave in the hallways
we know
in the soul depths
peace is possible

Remember a community of the book,
World Healing, World Peace
knowing spaciousness
in our hearts
healing is possible
now as we dance
life

Ann
J.
White

Amazed and inspired by her own life, Ann White has lived the life of a grasshopper buffeted about by wild winds, yet always landing safely and creating a home wherever she finds herself.

Highlights include working with astronaut Frank Borman, sharing a hot dog with Ross Perot, enjoying a coffee with Florida Governor Chiles, and attending a ballet with Imelda Marcos. Ann has also survived childhood sexual abuse, one terrorist coup, two burglaries, one rape and countless misadventures – making her grateful for each of life's moments.

An international management consultant, board certified family attorney, rabbi, grief counselor, and trauma chaplain – Ann has worn many professional hats.

These days she spends her time in her enchanted cottage and chicken farm by Lake Michigan in Sheboygan, Wisconsin with two very weird dogs and six quirky hens.

Ann is the author of *The Sacred Art of Dog Walking, Living with Spirit Energy, Code Red – a Stress Rx for Trauma Workers*, and *So You Want to Be a Radio Host*. She has also been featured in numerous anthologies. She is the co-owner of The Creating Calm Network Broadcasting and Publishing Group along with Kimberly Burnham.

Ann produces and hosts several programs on CCN as well as officiating weddings and distributing Young Living Essential Oils and It Works! Body Wraps.

You can find her at:
www.HealthandWellnessbyAnnJWhite.com
www.CreatingCalmNetwork.com

The Blessings of Living Alone

I was looking for love
Decades spent looking for love
Broken hearts, sleepless nights, tears and anguish
Maybe it is age
Or maybe a coming home to self
I no longer look for love
I am love
I love me and enjoy my company
I love sleeping alone in my bed and spreading out like a
sheet angel
I love waking up when I want
Eating when I want
Lights on or off
Heat high or cool
Lots of blankets and the air conditioner running
Cold pizza for breakfast
Ice cream for supper
No need to shave my legs
Saying no when I don't want to go
I laugh at my own jokes
I sing in the shower
Yes, I dance conga lines of one around my house

I Am Grateful

I am grateful for cosmos flowers
That grow with a wild beauty, untamed and bold to the
world
Yet, in a way so delicate
I am grateful for dandelions
That survive against all odds - from a sunny smile to a puff
of faerie magic
They blow their stardust into the wind
I am grateful for weeds that can crack the sidewalk
And scream to the world, "I did it, you can too!"
I am grateful for sea glass that tumbles about
Getting battered and bullied by the tides
And yet emerges with glorious hues and shapes to delight
the most jaded beach walker
I am grateful for rainy nights and blustery winds causing us
to repair to our homes
And snuggle in our beds, pulling our many covers over our
very tired heads
I am grateful for leaves covering my lawn – brilliant before
they die
Not my neighbors wanting me to rake when I wonder why
Why dispose of such bejeweled beauty that blankets the
garden as it waits for spring
I am grateful for hippies old and young who sing songs of
peace and love
Who don't bow down to laws of greed and corruption and
hate
I am grateful for the lotus flower that teaches us that from
the muck and mire

Or from our former existence, we too can blossom
into the beautiful creation we are meant to be
I am grateful for me, wrinkled and lumpy, battered and
bruised by the years,
Yet enjoying every moment of this wild ass journey called
life
This is my thanksgiving.

The Amazingness of Being

Damn!
The knife slipped
I cut my finger
Blood, blood, and more blood
The knife has germs from what I was cutting
My body bled them away
Soon the bleeding stopped and a scab formed
Each day I would watch my finger change
Each day, the miracle of my body transformed the cut
From the inside out
From a pink of soreness
To a deeper hue of healing.
A skinned knee
A splinter deeply embedded working its way out
An ingrown hair, wrapped in white cells and expelled
What an amazing creation we are that we take for granted
We eat and our bodies use what they need and eliminate the
rest
We sleep and our bodies restore
We make love and recreate
Yet how much time do we sit in awe of the miraculous
being we are?
I am grateful for my eyelashes and earwax
My fingernails and callouses that form to protect tender
skin
I am grateful for nose hair and saliva
For the blood coursing through my body
For my intestines doing their intestine-thing
For lungs to breathe in air and my heart that pumps my life
force
For slumber and dreams
For emotions of joy and tears
Excitement and all the nerves that pulse to create these
feelings

Synapses in my brain to create thought
Or create creations as a creative being
The ability to sing and dance and skip and shout
What an incredible being I am
I stand in awe and in gratitude of the miracle that is me.

Keith
Alan
Hamilton

~Keith Alan Hamilton~ is an Author who writes a spiritually philosophical blend of poetry and prose that's often further pictorialized with his Smartphone photography. Keith is the online publisher/editor of three blogs which includes The Hamilton Gallery ~ Online.com Blog, the Keith Alan Hamilton.com Blog and the NatureIQ.com Blog. Keith is also an exhibited artist, a fervent promoter of other artists and a professional Information Specialist/Investigator (Private/Corporate Sector – LPI).

Keith firmly believes, "The true act of creating art, is for it to be used for the everlasting benefit of all humanity" by using art to create change.

Driven by that belief, Keith's mission is within the spirit brought forth in his book series Nature ~ IQ: Let's Survive, Not Die! to see the value of proactively working together to improve the overall well-being of humanity. So people become more willing and able to help themselves and then do the same for others. To exemplify this mission a portion of the proceeds from the Keith's book series and his Art Store are donated to help support promising research into the cause, treatment, and management of MS, Fibromyalgia, Diabetes, Cancer, Hydrocephalus and mental conditions (Bipolar, Depression, Autism, etc.).

How Grateful

pass me the turkey
the dressing
the mashed potatoes
the gravy
how thankful
how grateful
are ya ~
for what you have ….
your family ~
or for being able
to have the chance
to do something
beyond the traditional
for someone else …..

give back more than you receive
and reap the blessing
of what you sow ~

peace and healing through love …..

I am not a saint

thank you I say
for another year
oh God I pray to thee
for the health and well-being
of my family
friends and neighbors
my fellow citizens
the world of human-kind
even my enemy
I am not a saint
just an everyday person
with a grateful spirit
and a heart full of hope

for all THE HUMAN RACE

peace and healing through love …..

the gift of deeds

I am the spiritual kind
a modern day mystic
of sorts .....
I ain't religious
but don't have a problem
with celebrating
Thanksgiving
being thankful is cool
I didn't say groovy
'cause that was just before
my generation
as I get older
I tend to
appreciate
what I have .....
but especially
the gift of deeds
I have done for another
fellow human being
regardless of
skin color
sex
gender
nationality
ethnicity
culture or belief

peace and healing through love .....

Katherine
Wyatt

Katherine Wyatt, born in Pittsburgh, PA., comes from a family of artists and writers that date back into the fifteen hundreds. Her mother was a cartoonist whose work was published globally. Her father was a writer in the corporate world, and he started his career as a journalist as a young man. Katherine was formally a ballet dancer who was trained at the prestigious School of American Ballet and danced the New York City Ballet repertoire for many years. She then went to college and got a BA and an MA in World Religions, and MA in Humanities and another MS in Instructional Design for Online Applications. She Attended Florida State University, among other. She then taught college students for three years. Katherine has written all of her life, but mostly academically until eight years ago. When she was seventeen she began a spiritual journey that led her around the world, and to Rishekesh, India. There she studied yoga in the tradition of the Himalayan Masters. She also has spent the last four years studying the history and traditions of Native Americans, and is still learning much in this area. With a strong background in the arts and her deep interest in spirituality her poetry often reflects the human connection to the divine. Her work is inspired by both eastern and western tradition. Katherine is currently and academic writer who loves to write poetry and has two books published.

Katherine's work can be found at Facebook as well
https://www.facebook.com/katherinewyatt.trinitypoetry

She can also be found at Reverbnation and SoundCloud
https://soundcloud.com/katherine-wyatt-trinity
http://www.reverbnation.com/katherinewyatt?profile_view
_source=header_icon_nav

~clearcut

There is a place in the bayous
smoothed by the scales of alligators
as they slide onto the land
seeking sunlight and food
it is where the wild things grow
Across the bayou
they are tearing down the trees
pulling off the skin of the Mother
there is no grass left
they will lay sod there
leaving a few noble oaks
for a pleasant view
Eighteen holes to play on
another one just like it only a mile away
Clearcut
pulling off Her skin
as the hippies gather round watching
protesting but unheard
So called "power" and influence
rarely heasr the voice
of something sacred
Who would be imprisoned if they peeled off the skin
of those in charge of "progress"?
Shunka, (dog), my Beloved and I
share breakfast on sacred soil
learn our song and walk barefoot
I wander down the gator trail to wash a necklace
in the bayous
It is primal ecstatic
to wash mud from between one's toes

My Beloved cooks millet and seeds
mixed with sautéed pears
Shunka shakes off the dust from his coat
We settle in for the day
And as sun sets I wonder
where the gators will go
when the men in plaid pants
with expensive golf clubs
tee off……

~sacred now

Trees hold deep roots into the ground..
…..reaching for the sky
blue sky written into my bones
as the sun and leaves paint my face in shadows
and shunka (Dog) and I wrestle and play
barefoot … as the trees grant us shade
from a blazing sun .. its rays
falling around us in spectrum colors
we cannot see, yet feel that magic
There is the beat of the drum..
echoing through the bayous
alive with its own voice.. a living being
in this sacred space
singing as we walk..…
Shunka running ahead stopping to see
if we are within eyeshot
dancing when we find a new alcove..
every moment ecstatic.. sacred
There is my love
long auburn hair and a black feather
soft yet strong like the trees..
barefoot we walk with shunka
I chase a butterfly or find a clearing
Sunstreams in rainbow pouring over us
I dance barefoot
in Sacred Space…..
a thousand faces in the trees
sing a song on the wind…
it echoes within…
I breathe …. trees exhale and I inhale'
Shunka takes point
.. as we walk forward
blissful in each NOW moment
…Sacred moment…. Precious day

~shifting flavors

I place my sundresses in the closet
searching for sleeved shirts and blue jeans
leaving a few strapped tops around
as the days shift from cool to sweltering...
settling into taciturn cold evenings
I warm cider on the stove with cinnamon sticks
as we feast on the gourds of fall
They are moving the horses again
the trailers go in and out at night
quarter horses are finished
as the thoroughbreds move in
I remain indifferent to that shift.........
We share tamarind soda,
amongst the rooted flavors of this season
of in betweens with its bipolar weather,
gentle shifts for the Now
There is a feeling of being alive in the heat of summer
giving way to a crisp clarity
as the cool air falls upon the fading tan of my shoulders
I try to be the poet... but am choosing to live
...poetry

Fahredin
Shehu

Born in Rahovec, South East of Kosova, in 1972. graduated at Prishtina University, Oriental Studies.

Actively works on Calligraphy discovering new mediums and techniques for this specific for of plastic art.

Certified expert in Andragogy/ Capacity Building, Training delivery, Coaching and Mentoring, Facilitating etc.

In last ten years he operated as Independent Scientific Researcher in the field of World Spiritual Heritage and Sacral Esthetics.

Fahredin Shehu is a highly *Noted* and *Acclaimed* World Renowned Poet, Author, Teacher and so much more. He graduated from Prishtina University with a Degree in Oriental Studies. In his continuing Education he received an M.A. in Literature. and a PhD in Sacral Esthetics.

Fahredin hails from Rahovec, South East of Kosova and has been embraced affectionately for his acutely gifted insightful poetic expressions by the Global Poetry Community. The depth and knowledge of many spiritual aspects that affect Humanity subtly shines through in his work. ***Pleroma's Dew & Maelstrom*** are very graceful works that serves to add to the accolades of this much celebrated Poet / Author / Philosopher.

http://www.innerchildpress.com/fahredin-shehu

The "I" who believes in now

Taming troubles I sow fear
to those who say:
"you listen to music
how dare you?"

…and those who dare not
to hear the sounds of fallen white rose
petals when the bee in a hush informs
the Calla Lily- the secret is mirrored on the dew.
This bears the timing of assembly.
We shall all meet before Souls
where the mists vanish and the day is bright.

After we pass the bridge
a goblet of vine with few blood- drops
sipped in to hail life and when I love
I really do until I faint- for the one who love
is different from the one who loves not.
The one who love once- faint in love
have difficulties to get unaccustomed,
for the "I" is the one who love
for eternity and a day more
Yet he blindly believes in "Now".

The Loom

Yet you are my dew in the petal of eternity

You've got few strings of mine
With their painted threads
You've set up the net
In your loom
For the tapestry of your last gammon

You are happy in this delusion
You enjoy your pace of life
While you believe
Others are blind

I'm not that bad to salute your illusion
Even in the moments when you think
You are the Queen of the city
That cooked the last blood supper
For the Peninsula of hatred.

Wake up three times I evoke
Don't let the abyss swallow
All your dreams and hopes
So the Divine may abandon you.

Hidden in the White Roses

open my chest if you want to see the rod of heaven's river,
while it strains in its bed,
where the white roses swim…

The hunger for beauty created canyons of longing for a
quantum of moment.

Again leaving is telling me thunder as melodeon, quiver of
veins and bones,
while I come to Thy meeting embarrassedly hide life's
broken toy, buried in human darkness; Alas you know my
pains, tears in blood percolated as black pressed grapes

While I swirled in the whirlpool of "I"-s, seeking for the
spark of the of Your sight

Remained deaf for the multitude of "THEM", and the
multitude of "US"

The moon is full, the moonlight feeds me while I listen
lullabys of Gabriel

To sleep the thirsty souls; the starmist flirts to my
appearance as it wishes to drop its mercy, at the pain
caused by human poison.

These words are arguments of the Threshold of the other
side where the describable forms and the audible voices
disappear, and the tongue knotted in nine knots.

The eye is stopping the sight to store its image in my consciousness.

Behold oh…"I" of the "US" while we rejoice within the White Roses and while we lick the pearly dews at dawn, and we smell the distant Neroli at dusk

While we celebrate life as cosmic minute that lasts for eternity and a day more.

~ ~ ~

…Neve na mungon vokabulari tokësor për çështje qiellore.

…We lack terrestrial vocabulary for the celestial quest

Hülya
N.
Yılmaz

hülya n. yılmaz was born and raised in Turkey but has been living in the U.S. as a university instructor since she earned her liberal arts doctoral degree from The University of Michigan. During her studies, she gave birth to her life source – a daughter who is now a mother herself. yılmaz authored a then groundbreaking research book in German on the literary reflections of cross-cultural interactions between the West and the Islamic East. She has a chapter published in a research book and presented her smaller scholarly projects at various national and international conferences. A few were published in academic journals.

A member of the Academy of American Poets, Dr. yılmaz authored with Inner Child Press, Ltd. her debut book, *Trance.* In this book of poetry in English, German and Turkish, hülya offers a venue for deliberations on identity formation and assertion within a multi-cultural context. Her narrations then alert readers to the urgent need for a re-visit to the often-unquestioned patriarchal mindset across the world. Several of her other creative work continue to appear in other Inner Child Press, Ltd. publications.

A licensed freelance writer and editor and a member of the Editorial Freelancers Association, hülya n. yılmaz served as editorial consultant for a large number of literary manuscripts, having published several book evaluations and critiques. She has also extensive experience in literary translations between English, German and Turkish in any direction – an example of which is present in *Trance.*

Links:
editorphd.hulyanyilmaz@gmail.com
www.writerandeditordryilmaz.com
www.authoroftrance.com
http://www.innerchildpress.com/hulyas-professional-writers-services.php
http://dolunaylaben.wordpress.com

Hülya N. Yılmaz

in our attempts to heal

of course i know it's a selfish act
but i do it all the same
not at all any differently than you

we are aware of their suffering and pain
yet sigh in relief for we are safe
we may shed a tear perhaps two
post a fiery message or so
even go as far as dropping a note...

we think we help ease their agony
that arrogant is how we can get
all along reacting from outside
hardly from a point of within
spelling out thanks
behind masks of loud shapes and sizes

i can almost hear you pout

well...

the spotlight's on us now with no doubt

forgive me today for my biting tongue
i guess i just have heard one too many...
to pretend to heed the command for calm

let's think about this one more time...

who is this "they" you say?

all but the "we" we evermore claim to be

an old tune

a beloved song in my memory's ears
utters the wisdom of the aching hopeful

"i too had my sorrows
joys not granted to many
ready also to be forgotten
life you have my thanks"

regaining gratitude for the ills
for their trust in the i on its brink of giving up
lending it eyes of the unseen kind
guiding it to its forgotten core
leading it to the gems all around
in a world of marvel moving about
thankfully in disregard of the selfish self

happiness

lies within…

the one-way swing of the pendulum

grab it

be thankful when you can

Teresa
E.
Gallion

Teresa E. Gallion was born in Shreveport, Louisiana and moved to Illinois at the age of 15. She completed her undergraduate training at the University of Illinois Chicago and received her master's degree in Psychology from Bowling Green State University in Ohio. She retired from New Mexico state government in 2012.

She moved to New Mexico in 1987. While writing sporadically for many years, in 1998 she started reading her work in the local Albuquerque poetry community. She has been a featured reader at local coffee houses, bookstores, art galleries, museums, libraries, Outpost Performance Space, the Route 66 Festival in 2001 and the State of Oklahoma's Poetry Festival in Cheyenne, Oklahoma in 2004. She occasionally hosts an open mic.

Teresa's work is published in numerous Journals and anthologies. She has two CDs: *On the Wings of the Wind* and *Poems from Chasing Light*. She has published three books: *Walking Sacred Ground, Contemplation in the High Desert* and *Chasing Light.*

Chasing Light was a finalist in the 2013 New Mexico/Arizona Book Awards.

The surreal high desert landscape and her personal spiritual journey influence the writing of this Albuquerque poet. When she is not writing, she is committed to hiking the enchanted landscapes of New Mexico. You may preview her work at ***http://bit.ly/1aIVPNq*** or ***http://bit.ly/13IMLGh***

Oak Creek

The heartbeat of Sedona is Oak Creek.
Small in physical stature,
grand in spiritual upliftment,

flows with healing energy
to stimulate the body, tease the senses,
excites with the dance
of light and sound on water.

My friend paints at the creek.
Pure joy from her eyelids
spills over a white canvas,
swells into an image of cathedral rock.

I sit my feet in the morning water,
feel peace stream through my body.
The water releases my fever,
relaxes every piece of me.

A new day, a new beginning,
in the cold clarity of water
that captures a thankful
moment of simple breath.

Side of Morning

As I walk into the side of morning
the sun cuts my ankles,
water runs down my face, back and legs.

The wind creates cool tickles on moist skin.
I feel ecstatic with such a natural massage.
Sometimes the self-talk asks,

why are you smiling?
It is good for the heart.
Nature designed as a labor of love

waits for you to partake.
Her vast canvas is available
for all who want to see.

Gratefulness expands my chest
for the gift of walking
in the quiet shadows of morning.

Cumulus Clouds

Today the sun's glow
teases the open road.
A smile overtakes my face,
a lax hold on the stern wheel,
eyes target the sky.

I want to walk on cumulus.
The pull is so powerful,
I almost lose the road.
Second instinct kicks in

brings my eyes back to the road.
But I wade in the ecstasy
of no time and space
and the clouds beckon with
a stairway on the distant horizon.

My inner child floats on air waves,
teases me with a come join me grin.
I wonder what it would feel like
to walk on cumulus clouds?

William
S.
Peters Sr.

Bill's writing career spans a period quickly approaching 50 years. Being first Published in 1972, Bill has since went on to Author 28 additional Volumes of Poetry, Short Stories, etc., expressing his thoughts on matters of the Heart, Spirit, Consciousness and Humanity. His primary focus is that of Love, Peace and Understanding!

Bill is the Founding Director of Inner Child Enterprises as well as the Past Director of Publicity for Society Hill Music.

Bill says . . .

I have always likened Life to that of a Garden. So, for me, Life is simply about the Seeds we Sow and Nourish. All things we "Think and Do", will "Be" Cause and eventually manifest itself to being an "Effect" within our own personal "Existences" and "Experiences" . . . whether it be Fruit, Flowers, Weeds or Barren Landscapes! Bill highly regards the Fruits of his Labor and wishes that everyone would thus go on to plant "Lovely" Seeds on "Good Ground" in their own Gardens of Life!

to connect with Bill, he is all things Inner Child :
www.iaminnerchild.com

Personal Web Site
www.iamjustbill.com

every time

if i could write the words
to make the pages of my book
breathe,
i would

 i wish you to turn the pages
of your vicarious life
with a fervor
that you may experience
this depth i feel
about our lives

i want my feelings
to metamorphose to thoughts, to words
that touch your heart
and fill your breast
with inspiration
that you may be moved,
and pay if ahead of your self
and move another

let my phrasing dance into your dreams
that you may live larger
than your expectations
and we will hold hands
and "skip to the loo"
through the verses
of promise , wonder and intrigue

may there be no conclusions,
no end

may the journey be "never ending"
as our smiles

adorn our face
with a knowing
that our goodness is deserved

if i could but write the words
that entices you
to open your arms
and seek another soul
to embrace
as if it is your long lost self
you have been searching for
since inception, since birth

if i could but write the words
if i could but write the words
i would . . . every time

i am !

my Breath is One
my Heartbeat is One
my Pulse is One
with the manifestation of creation

i am but a single note
in the orchestrated symphony
we call life

i am my own autonomous melody
seeking to harmonize
in this performance
and it is my consciousness
that differentiates
betwixt the illusion, delusion
and the reality
of my attachment

there is birth,
there is death
and all endings yield
to new beginnings

"i lay down my life that i may pick it up again, for i have
the power to do so"
that "i" is who ""I Am",
who you are,
who we are

for . . .
our Breath is One
our Heartbeat is One
our Pulse is One
with the manifestation of creation

'i am' but a single note
in the orchestrated symphony
we call life
and i am the Conductor,
the Instrument,
the Orchestra,
the Music

i am !

who am i

who am i
that looks upon thy beauty
and attempt to veil it
with my ignorance

who am i
to stand in the presence of magnificence
found in a blossoming flower
and not acknowledge it's beauty

who am i
to not listen to the whisperings
of the babbling brook
or the stream
or the river
or the ocean
or the rain
and not take heed
to the consciousness
that assists in my awakening

who am i
that remains silent
when the ills of men
assault our divinity

who am i
to refuse embrace
of my brothers and sisters
in love

who am i
to not reach out my hand
when my beloved is in need

who am i
to rebuke the ideas and dreams
of others,
regardless of the smallness
of my own visions

who am i
to not respect the Mother of life
and cast my waste upon her
while plundering her depths

who am i
to espouse voices of disdain
and malcontent
against perfection

who am i
that can not admit
that i have wavered
along the road,
casting my faith
to perdition
because of my lack of sight

who am i
that picks up arms
and gives cause for others
to follow me

who am i
to turn away
from the smiles of the children
who give them without reservation

who am i
to close my heart
when so many are in need
of but a little love

who am i
to reject the perspectives
of others,
for in consideration
i too may discover a pot of gold

who am i
to damn my own soul
by not living
the celestial holy life
for which i was created

who am i
to ignore creations music
and hold my self back
from dancing

who am i
to deny any of these aspects
of the face of God
which calls to my greater self
to live beyond vicariousness

who am i
who are you ?

November 2015

Features

~ * ~

Alan W. Jankowski
Bismay Mohanty
James Moore

Alan
W.
Jankowski

Alan W. Jankowski is the award winning author of well over one hundred short stories, plays and poems. His stories have been published online, and in various journals including Oysters & Chocolate, Muscadine Lines: A Southern Journal, eFiction Magazine, Zouch, The Rusty Nail, and a few others he can't remember at the moment. His poetry has more recently become popular, and his 9-11 Tribute poem was used extensively in ceremonies starting with the tenth anniversary of this tragic event...

http://www.storiesspace.com/forum/yaf_postst538_My-911-Tribute-poem-has-been-in-print-at-least-fourteen-times-in-2011.aspx

He currently has one book out on Inner Child Press titled "I Often Wonder: a collection of poetry and prose." It is available directly from Inner Child at this link...
http://www.innerchildpress.com/alan-w-jankowski.php

When he is not writing, which is not often, his hobbies include music and camera collecting. He currently resides in New Jersey. He always appreciates feedback of any kind on his work, and can be reached by e-mail at: Exakta66@gmail.com

Let Me Be The One

When life hands you so much sorrow and pain,
And takes so much with little to gain,
You're like a train that somehow left the track,
Can we ever get the good times back?

Do you recall when the world was so new?
And there seemed no limit to what we could do,
Harking back to those simpler times,
Of children's books and nursery rhymes.

Can you remember those simple joys?
Childhood dreams and children's toys,
How did we ever lose our way?
Can we ever get back to that day?

Yet somehow those dreams all have faded,
Have we really become that jaded?
The only cure for lost love is a love that's new,
The only love that matters is a love that's true.

And here we are, two souls destined to meet,
Why should we ever accept defeat?
For us our lives have just begun,
We can do this together, let me be the one.

The Letter

I poured out every thought upon the page,
Filling it up with all the rage and anger,
That you have instilled inside me.
My pen literally quivered,
As I held it in my sweaty hand,
Yet the words flowed swiftly,
As venomous as any snake,
And almost as deadly.
As I poured the last of the wine into my glass,
I reviewed my handiwork.
Three pages of anger.
Three pages of hurt.
An expression of all you've done to me,
As best as I possibly could.
I carefully folded the letter,
And stuffed it in the envelope.
And with quivering pen,
I wrote out your address.
It was late, and I'd post it in the morning.
I went off to bed that night.
The next day I spent quietly around the house.
It was cold outside,
And it was warm by the fire.
In the afternoon,
I opened another bottle of wine.
I sat pensively for some time,
Just watching the flames dance
Upon the logs in the fireplace.
Amidst the crackling of the timbers,
I picked up the envelope.
I stare down at your name upon it.
I take another sip of wine,
And remove the letter.

As I begin to read it again,
I am reminded of everything you've ever done.
All the hurt you've caused,
To myself and my family,
Comes back again over three pages.
My blood starts to boil again,
And my palms start to sweat.
There is a damp thumbprint on the page,
And the edges of the letter are damp and frayed,
From holding it tightly in my hands.
I lean back in my chair.
I know I am not ready to forgive.
I don't know that I ever will be.
And God knows I will never forget.
In fact, I hope you rot in Hell,
And if I could deliver you there myself,
Lord knows, I would.
But, I can never stoop to your level.
I can never stoop to your level.
I sit for some time just watching the fire.
In a while, I pick up the letter,
And walk over to the fireplace.
I toss it upon the flames.
I sit back down and sip my wine.
And as I watch the letter burn,
The sparks crackling,
And the black soot fall upon the logs,
I know I can never stoop to your level,
But, there's a part of me that says to myself,
"God, I wish that letter were you."

Accept Me As I Am

I never meant to take you for granted,
Because you're the best I've found,
I truly cherish every moment,
Of the times you are around.

But now and then we say and do,
Things we don't intend,
My actions were just misconstrued,
I never meant to offend.

We all regret from time to time,
Things we do and say,
I just wish I could turn back time,
And take your pain away.

You mean so much more to me,
Than my actions can ever show,
I would never intentionally hurt you,
This I want you to know.

Sometimes we hurt the ones we love most,
But that never was my plan,
I just hope you can forgive me,
And accept me as I am.

Alan W. Jankowski

Bismay
Mohanty

Bismay Mohanty, a poet of international fame from India, is the youngest poet to be featured in Year of the Poet-II January edition. Currently doing his in graduation Computer Science and Engineering, he is quite active in literary sessions.

Writing poems since the fourth grade, Bismay says, "The reason behind everything big is always small. The tiniest of thoughts can give rise to the greatest imaginations of beauty and inspiration. It is the work of a poet to bring magic into words and give life to the world of imaginations."

His works cover aspects of romance, nature, human tendency, society and inspiration.

He can be mailed at bismaymohanty.97@gmail.com

DON'T KNOW

Don't know how long life is.
Don't know till when I will live.
Don't know of my home after death.
Don't know what all I will leave.
Don't know if I would be happy then.
Don't know if all but me.
Don't know I will be damned.
Don't know if allowed to infinity.
Don't know if it will be helpful.
So ignorant am I?

The Culprit

A name that lionized once
Exemplifying crystal goodness
Dwindles now amidst the crowd
For an instinct extravagance
Who loved once, now fear
The name that lies in darkness.

'The culprit' now reminisces
All that made his past.
Endurance long did he face but
Long didn't his freedom last.
Joy comes slow and with struggle
Folly! He wanted it fast.

The culprit earlier envied people
With love, money and other wealth
Unlike winners, he failed to stand alone
In himself he did lose faith.
Burning desires made evil rhetorical
Pity the age evil ignite stealth.

Forbidden fruits he dared to reach
Stranger he felt on being a deuce.
He cherished at the illusion
Of walking on a supreme avenue.
Everything comes with a price, he forget
Now the Devil waited for his revenue.

Blindfolded by the espy of interim wealth
Wealth of humanity has become a fiction.
Just of the self he kept ruminating on
Never thought of the innocent's malediction
He who snatched several dreams by his desire
Awaited for him the much deserved destination.

In his cell, his sleep now breaks
As the moonlight seeks him in murky.
The joy in seasons are lost forever
Burning passions depleted of intensity
Time passed with thoughts of past and future
Alas! Immature insanity changed his destiny.

The Lonesome Tree on the Hill

Many times my eyes attract
The sight of a tree on a distant hill.
My visualization makes me haunted
By a silence and a thundering feel.

There it stands a little below the peak
Leafless and lifeless it stands upright.
Surrounded by tiny dried bushes it depicts
Massiveness alone does not give delight.

A ghost of loneliness surrounds
As an eyes among the blinds.
What gusto lies in grandeur?
If satisfaction is what self deprives.

Having observed the tree much
My mind explodes contemplating
What if I live such a life where
Hardwork without interest goes failing.

I have ever thought it wise
To opt for the road not taken.
Now that it's time to return to the junction
May future whiten the days gone blacken.

Bismay Mohanty

James
Moore

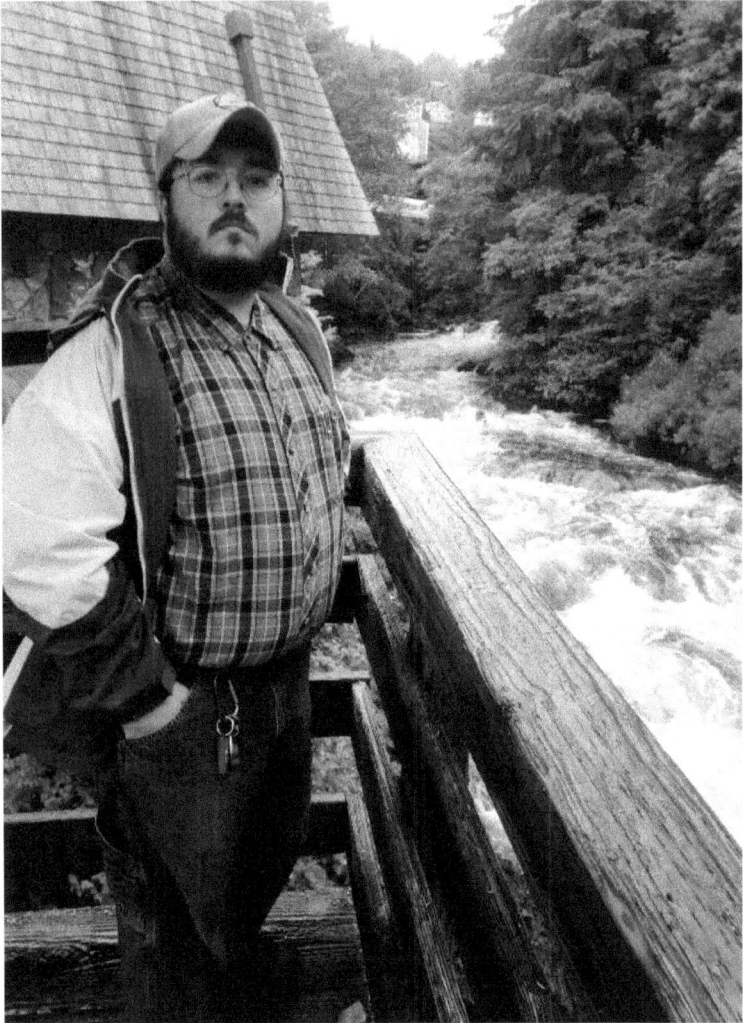

James Moore, born in Virginia, comes into poetry with a love of the word. Most recently inspired by Sylvia Plath, Charles Bukowski, and a steady diet of low rent movies and episodes of the show *It's Always Sunny in Philadelphia*, James tries to create the positive with the irreverent; his poems represent the art in the soul of a young man hoping to bring a new vision into the world...

A few things have changed since James was last inside the Year of the Poet—he no longer waits tables, but now he trudges on as a cashier at a Martin's Food Store, where some customers mistake him for Michael Madson (Mr. Blonde from *Reservoir Dogs*). He is about to transfer into a four-year college and finish out his degree, moving on to grad school and a new fishing boat. Somewhere along the line some dates were dropped. The wind blows. The dog howls long into the night.

Lately James has been playing with romantic, religious and personal themes in his poems; as evidenced by the current sampling, James is developing his sense of well being in the mode of the Valentine. If Scarlett Johansson ever comes across these poems, tell her to give this guy a call...

James is still working on some crime scripts, and reading back issues of Harvey Pekar's AMERICAN SPLENDOR. Coke is still the best cocktail in existence, and *The Tick* is still an underrated TV show. Life is good, don't waste it he says...

Why I Write

Some nights
you dream of
painting
your life story
when the fire will not

sustain you long
enough for you
to cleanse yourself

of the dark hours
what eat at you
constantly.

I don't
possess the will
for the canvas,
but the words do
make the work
do itself in
other ways,

other avenues
which tempt me
to come back
from the fantasy
and into the

flame

A Little Love Poem

the night and the soul
have been intertwined;

I've needed the time
just to center myself
and of course now I've
realized the whole

secret to both the
universe and my-
self: she was the

one, my moon
princess and my

sweetness coming

into my life so
gently I feel like
I finally know

who God really
is tonight.

The Choice

She builds for me
this one carefully crafted puzzle
before I am allowed to head

back home—"behind the
one door lies the dream you
remember tomorrow morning;
the other a dream you feel

just on the tip
of your tongue,

waiting

for you to speak
it's name."

For me it is no
real choice…I've made for
myself only one passage
back home, that being

all that is built
within her embrace.

Other

Anthological

works from

Inner Child Press, ltd.

www.innerchildpress.com

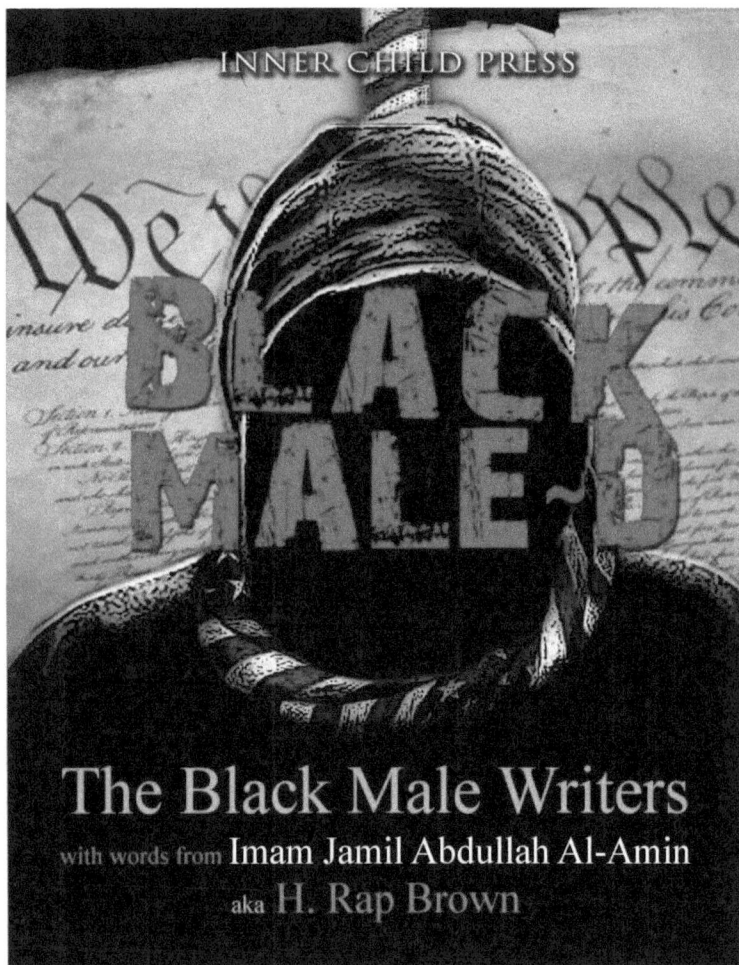

The Black Male Writers

with words from Imam Jamil Abdullah Al-Amin

aka H. Rap Brown

The Year of the Poet II

November 2015

Featured Poets
Alan W. Jankowski
Bismay Mohanty
James Moore

Topaz

The Poetry Posse 2015

Jamie Bond * Gail Weston Shazor * Albert 'Infinite' Carrasco
Siddartha Beth Pierce * Janet P. Caldwell * Tony Henninger
Joe DaVerbal Minddancer * Neetu Wali * Shareef Abdur – Rasheed
Kimberly Burnham * Ann White * Keith Alan Hamilton
Katherine Wyatt * Fahredin Shehu * Hülya N. Yılmaz
Teresa E. Gallion * Jackie Allen * William S. Peters, Sr.

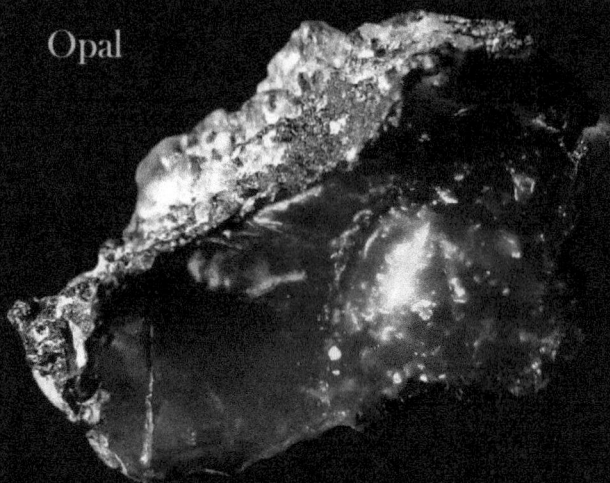

The Year of the Poet II
October 2015

Featured Poets
Monte Smith * Laura J. Wolfe * William Washington

Opal

The Poetry Posse 2015
Jamie Bond * Gail Weston Shazor * Albert 'Infinite' Carrasco
Siddartha Beth Pierce * Janet P. Caldwell * Tony Henninger
Joe DaVerbal Minddancer * Neetu Wali * Shareef Abdur – Rasheed
Kimberly Burnham * Ann White * Keith Alan Hamilton
Katherine Wyatt * Fahredin Shehu * Hülya N. Yılmaz
Teresa E. Gallion * Jackie Allen * William S. Peters, Sr.

The Year of the Poet II

September 2015

Featured Poets

Alfreda Ghee   Lonneice Weeks Badley   Demetrios Trifiatis

Sapphires

The Poetry Posse 2015

Jamie Bond * Gail Weston Shazor * Albert 'Infinite' Carrasco
Siddartha Beth Pierce * Janet P. Caldwell * Tony Henninger
Joe DaVerbal Minddancer * Neetu Wali * Shareef Abdur – Rasheed
Kimberly Burnham * Ann White * Keith Alan Hamilton
Katherine Wyatt * Fahredin Shehu * Hülya N. Yılmaz
Teresa E. Gallion * Jackie Allen * William S. Peters, Sr.

The Year of the Poet II

August 2015

Peridot

Featured Poets

Gayle Howell

Ann Chalasz

Christopher Schultz

The Poetry Posse 2015

Jamie Bond * Gail Weston Shazor * Albert 'Infinite' Carrasco
Siddartha Beth Pierce * Janet P. Caldwell * Tony Henninger
Joe DaVerbal Minddancer * Neetu Wali * Shareef Abdur – Rasheed
Kimberly Burnham * Ann White * Keith Alan Hamilton
Katherine Wyatt * Fahredin Shehu * Hülya N. Yılmaz
Teresa E. Gallion * Jackie Allen * William S. Peters, Sr.

The Year of the Poet II

July 2015

The Featured Poets for July 2015

Abhik Shome * Christina Neal * Robert Neal

Rubies

The Poetry Posse 2015

Jamie Bond * Gail Weston Shazor * Albert 'Infinite' Carrasco
Siddartha Beth Pierce * Janet P. Caldwell * Tony Henninger
Joe DaVerbal Minddancer * Neetu Wali * Shareef Abdur – Rasheed
Kimberly Burnham * Ann White * Keith Alan Hamilton
Katherine Wyatt * Fahredin Shehu * Hülya N. Yılmaz
Teresa E. Gallion * Jackie Allen * William S. Peters, Sr.

The Year of the Poet II

June 2015

June's Featured Poets

Anahit Arustamyan * Yvette D. Murrell * Regina A. Walker

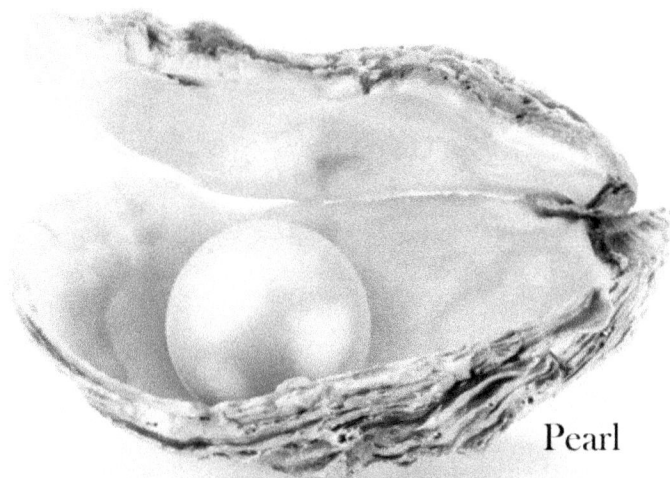

Pearl

The Poetry Posse 2015

Jamie Bond * Gail Weston Shazor * Albert 'Infinite' Carrasco
Siddartha Beth Pierce * Janet P. Caldwell * Tony Henninger
Joe DaVerbal Minddancer * Neetu Wali * Shareef Abdur – Rasheed
Kimberly Burnham * Ann White * Keith Alan Hamilton
Katherine Wyatt * Fahredin Shehu * Hülya N. Yılmaz
Teresa E. Gallion * Jackie Allen * William S. Peters, Sr.

The Year of the Poet II

May 2015

May's Featured Poets

Geri Algeri

Akin Mosi Chinnery

Anna Jakubcza

Emeralds

The Poetry Posse 2015

Jamie Bond * Gail Weston Shazor * Albert 'Infinite' Carrasco
Siddartha Beth Pierce * Janet P. Caldwell * Tony Henninger
Joe DaVerbal Minddancer * Neetu Wali * Shareef Abdur – Rasheed
Kimberly Burnham * Ann White * Keith Alan Hamilton
Katherine Wyatt * Fahredin Shehu * Hülya N. Yılmaz
Teresa E. Gallion * Jackie Allen * William S. Peters, Sr.

The Year of the Poet II
April 2015

Celebrating International Poetry Month

Our Featured Poets

Raja Williams * Dennis Ferado * Laure Charazac

Diamonds

The Poetry Posse 2015

Jamie Bond * Gail Weston Shazor * Albert 'Infinite' Carrasco
Siddartha Beth Pierce * Janet P. Caldwell * Tony Henninger
Joe DaVerbal Minddancer * Neetu Wali * Shareef Abdur – Rasheed
Kimberly Burnham * Ann White * Keith Alan Hamilton
Katherine Wyatt * Fahredin Shehu * Hülya N. Yılmaz
Teresa E. Gallion * Jackie Allen * William S. Peters, Sr.

The Year of the Poet II

March 2015

Our Featured Poets

Heung Sook * Anthony Arnold * Alicia Poland

Bloodstone

The Poetry Posse 2015

Jamie Bond * Gail Weston Shazor * Albert 'Infinite' Carrasco
Siddartha Beth Pierce * Janet P. Caldwell * Tony Henninger
Joe DaVerbal Minddancer * Neetu Wali * Shareef Abdur – Rasheed
Kimberly Burnham * Ann White * Keith Alan Hamilton
Katherine Wyatt * Fahredin Shehu * Hülya N. Yılmaz
Teresa E. Gallion * Jackie Allen * William S. Peters, Sr.

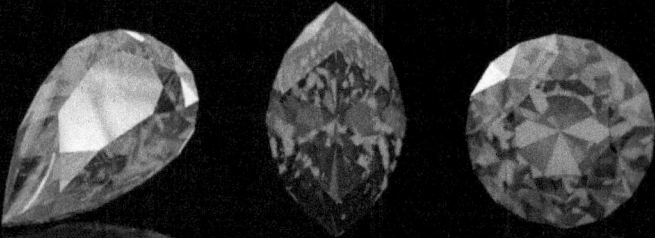

January 2015

Garnet

The Poetry Posse

Jamie Bond
Gail Weston Shazor
Albert 'Infinite' Carrasco
Siddartha Beth Pierce
Janet P. Caldwell
Tony Henninger
Joe Davis bal Mindancer
Robert Gibbons
Neetu Wali
Shareef Abdur – Rasheed
Kimberly Burnham
Ann White
Keith Alan Hamilton
Katherine Wyatt
Fahredin Shehu
Hülya N. Yılmaz
Teresa E. Gallion
Jackie Allen
William S. Peters, Sr.

January Feature Poets

Bismay Mohanti * Jen Walls * Eric Judah

The Year of the Poet

December 2014

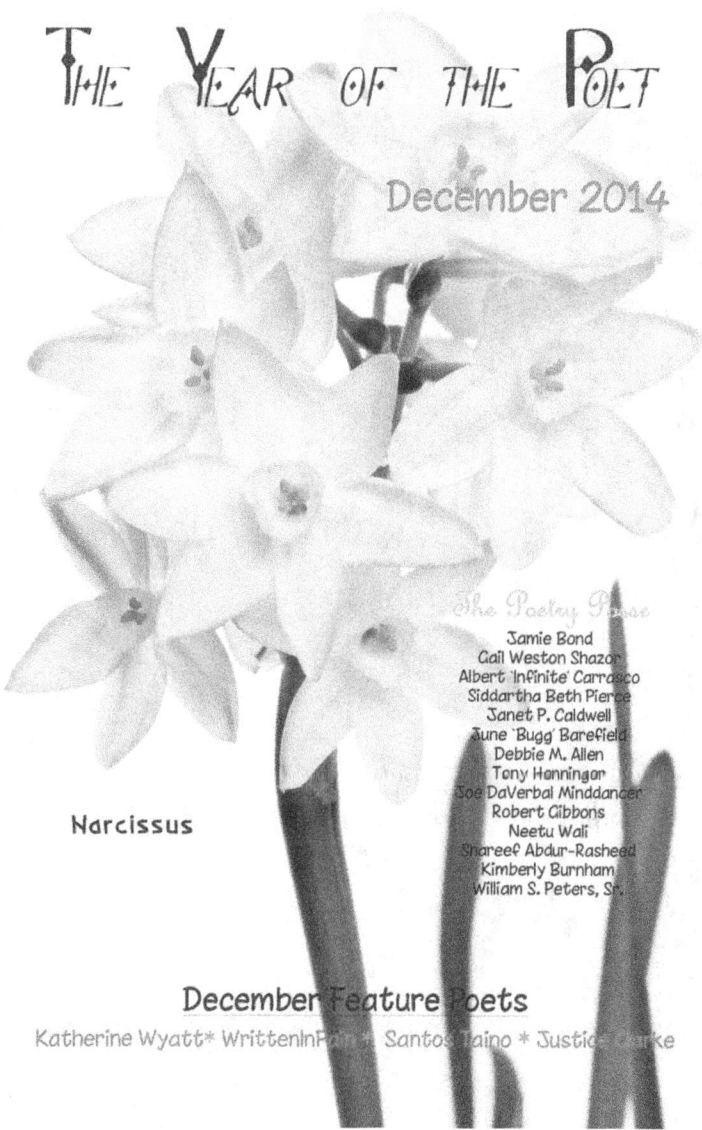

The Poetry Posse

Jamie Bond
Gail Weston Shazor
Albert 'Infinite' Carrasco
Siddartha Beth Pierce
Janet P. Caldwell
June 'Bugg' Barefield
Debbie M. Allen
Tony Henninger
Joe DaVerbal Minddancer
Robert Gibbons
Neetu Wali
Shareef Abdur-Rasheed
Kimberly Burnham
William S. Peters, Sr.

Narcissus

December Feature Poets

Katherine Wyatt* WritteninPain * Santos Jaino * Justice Clarke

THE YEAR OF THE POET

November 2014

Chrysanthemum

The Poetry Posse

Jamie Bond * Gail Weston Shazor * Albert 'Infinite' Carrasco * Siddartha Beth Pierce
Janet P. Caldwell * June 'Bugg' Barefield * Debbie M. Allen * Tony Henninger
Joe DaVerbal Minddancer * Robert Gibbons * Neetu Wali * Shareef Abdur-Rasheed
Kimberly Burnham * William S. Peters, Sr.

November Feature Poets

Jocelyn Mosman * Jackie Allen * James Moore * Neville Hiatt

THE YEAR OF THE POET

October 2014

Red Poppy

The Poetry Posse

Jamie Bond * Gail Weston Shazor * Albert 'Infinite' Carrasco * Siddartha Beth Pierce
Janet P. Caldwell * June 'Bugg' Barefield * Debbie M. Allen * Tony Henninger
Joe DaVerbal Minddancer * Robert Gibbons * Neetu Wali * Shareef Abdur-Rasheed
Kimberly Burnham * William S. Peters, Sr.

October Feature Poets

Ceri Naz * Rajendra Padhi * Elizabeth Castillo

The Year of the Poet

September 2014

Aster   Morning-Glory

Wild Charm of September Birthday Flower

September Feature Poets

Florence Malone * Keith Alan Hamilton

The Poetry Posse

Jamie Bond * Gail Weston Shazor * Albert 'Infinite' Carrasco * Siddartha Beth Pierce
Janet P. Caldwell * June 'Bugg' Barefield * Debbie M. Allen * Tony Henninger
Joe DaVerbal Minddancer * Robert Gibbons * Neetu Wali * Shareef Abdur-Rasheed
Kimberly Burnham * William S. Peters, Sr.

The Year of the Poet

August 2014

Gladiolus

The Poetry Posse

Jamie Bond
Gail Weston Shazor
Albert 'Infinite' Carrasco
Siddartha Beth Pierce
Janet P. Caldwell
June 'Bugg' Barefield
Debbie M. Allen
Tony Henninger
Joe DaVerbal Minddancer
Robert Gibbons
Neetu Wali
Shareef Abdur-Rasheed
Kimberly Burnham
William S. Peters, Sr.

August Feature Poets

Ann White * Rosalind Cherry * Sheila Jenkins

The Year of the Poet

July 2014

July Feature Poets

Christena A. V. Williams
Dr. John R. Strum
Kolade Olanrewaju Freedom

The Poetry Posse

Jamie Bond
Gail Weston Shazor
Albert 'Infinite' Carrasco
Siddartha Beth Pierce
Janet P. Caldwell
June 'Bugg' Barefield
Debbie M. Allen
Tony Henninger
Joe DaVerbal Minddancer
Robert Gibbons
Neetu Wali
Shareef Abdur-Rasheed
Kimberly Burnham
William S. Peters, Sr

Lotus
Asian Flower of the Month

the Year of the Poet

June 2014

Love & Relationship

Rose

June's Featured Poets

Shantelle McLin
Jacqueline D. E. Kennedy
Abraham N. Benjamin

The Poetry Posse

Jamie Bond
Gail Weston Shazor
Albert 'Infinite' Carrasco
Siddartha Beth Pierce
Janet P. Caldwell
June 'Bugg' Barefield
Debbie M. Allen
Tony Henninger
Joe DaVerbal Minddancer
Robert Gibbons
Neetu Wali
Shareef Abdur-Rasheed
Kimberly Burnham
William S. Peters, Sr.

the year of the poet

May 2014

May's Featured Poets

ReeCee
Joski the Poet
Shannon Stanton

Dedicated To our Children

The Poetry Posse

Jamie Bond
Gail Weston Shazor
Albert 'Infinite' Carrasco
Siddartha Beth Pierce
Janet P. Caldwell
June 'Bugg' Barefield
Debbie M. Allen
Tony Henninger
Joe DeVerbal Minddancer
Robert Gibbons
Neetu Wali
Shareef Abdur-Rasheed
Kimberly Burnham
William S. Peters, Sr.

Lily of the Valley

the Year of the Poet

April 2014

The Poetry Posse

Jamie Bond
Gail Weston Shazor
Albert 'Infinite' Carrasco
Siddartha Beth Pierce
Janet P. Caldwell
June 'Bugg' Barefield
Debbie M. Allen
Tony Henninger
Joe DeVerbal Minddancer
Robert Gibbons
Neetu Wali
Shareef Abdur-Rasheed
Kimberly Burnham
William S. Peters. Sr.

Our April Featured Poets

Fahredin Shehu
Martina Reisz Newberry
Justin Blackburn
Monte Smith

celebrating international poetry month

Sweet Pea

the Year of the Poet

The Poetry Posse

Jamie Bond
Gail Weston Shazor
Albert 'Infinite' Carrasco
Siddartha Beth Pierce
Janet P. Caldwell
June 'Bugg' Barefield
Debbie M. Allen
Tony Henninger
Joe DaVerbal Minddancer
Robert Gibbons
Neetu Wali
Shareef Abdur-Rasheed
Kimberly Burnham
William S. Peters, Sr.

March 2014

daffodil

Our March Featured Poets

Alicia C. Cooper & hülya yılmaz

the Year of the Poet

February 2014

violets

The Poetry Posse

Jamie Bond
Gail Weston Shazor
Albert 'Infinite' Carrasco
Siddartha Beth Pierce
Janet P, Caldwell
June 'Bugg' Barefield
Debbie M. Allen
Tony Henninger
Joe DaVerbal Minddancer
Robert Gibbons
Neetu Wali
Shareef Abdur-Rasheed
William S. Peters, Sr.

Our February Features

Teresa E. Gallion & Robert Gibson

The Year of the Poet
January 2014

The Poetry Posse

Jamie Bond
Gail Weston Shazor
Albert 'Infinite' Carrasco
Siddartha Beth Pierce
Janet P. Caldwell
June 'Bugg' Barefield
Debbie M. Allen
Tony Henninger
Joe DaVerbal Minddancer
Robert Gibbons
Neetu Wali
Shareef Abdur-Rasheed
William S. Peters, Sr.

Carnation

Our January Feature
Terri L. Johnson

Mandela

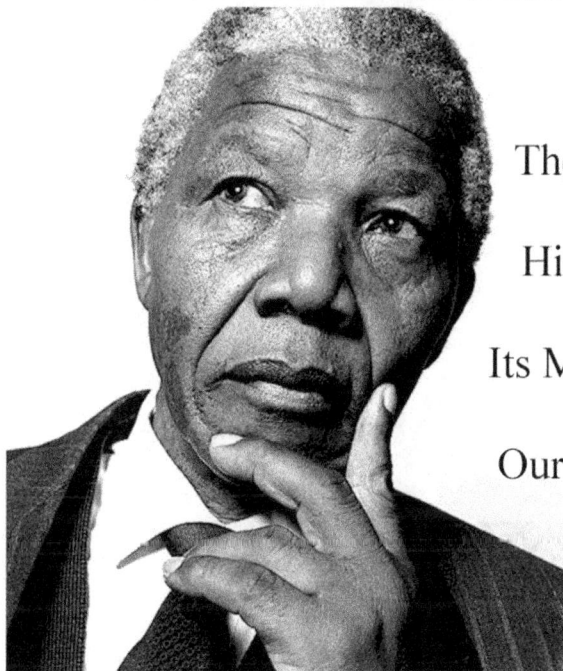

The Man

His Life

Its Meaning

Our Words

Poetry . . . Commentary & Stories
The Anthological Writers

A GATHERING OF WORDS

POETRY & COMMENTARY
FOR
TRAYVON MARTIN

World Healing
World Peace

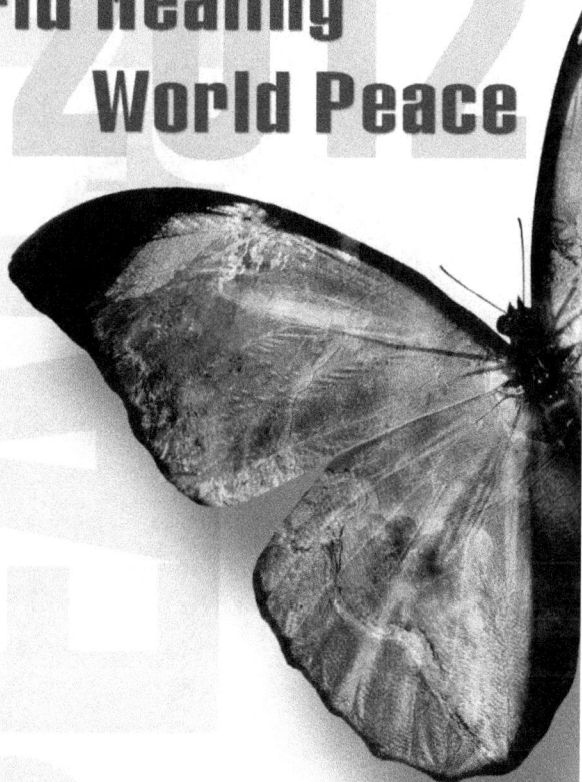

A POETRY ANTHOLOGY
Volume 1

Inner Child Press Anthologies

2012

World Healing
World Peace

A POETRY ANTHOLOGY
Volume 2

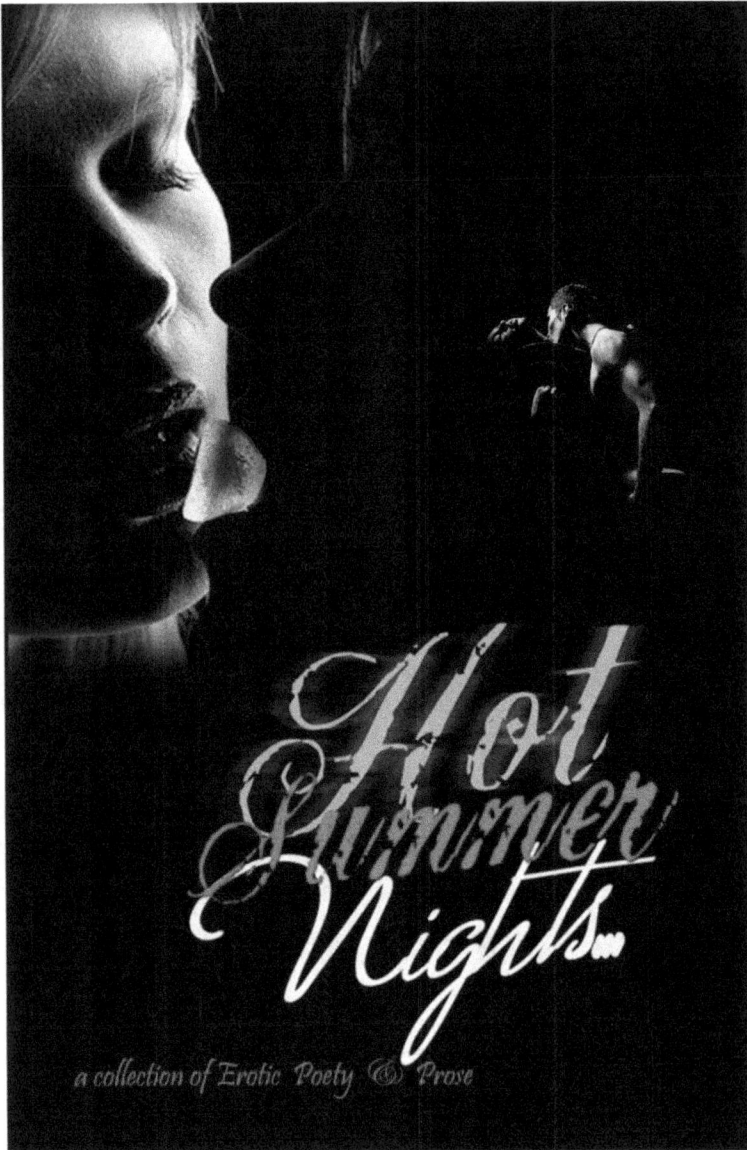

Hot Summer Nights...

a collection of Erotic Poetry & Prose

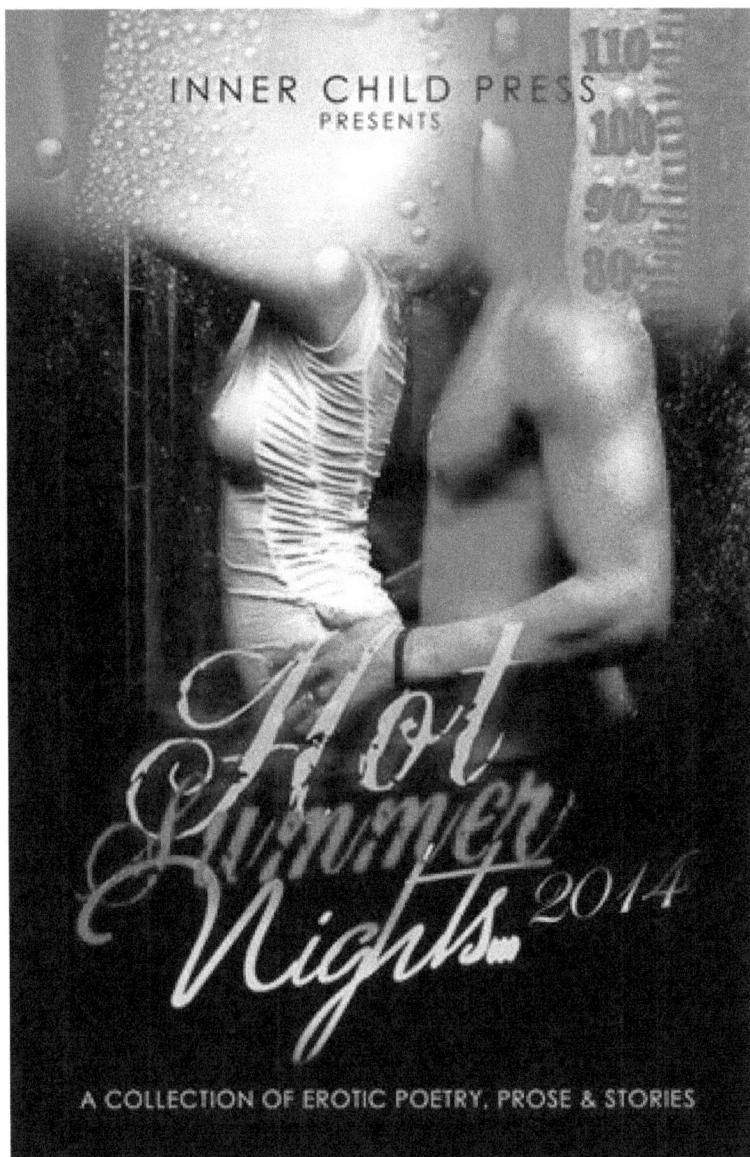

INNER CHILD PRESS
PRESENTS

Hot
Summer
Nights... 2014

A COLLECTION OF EROTIC POETRY, PROSE & STORIES

the

Valentine's Day

Anthology

poetry . . . prose & stories of love

The Love Writers

♡

i

want my

PoEtRy

to . . .

a collection of the Voices of Many inspired by …

Monte Smith

Inner Child Press Anthologies

a collection of the Voices of Many inspired by . . .

Monte Smith

want my

PoEtRy

to . . .

volume II

11 Words

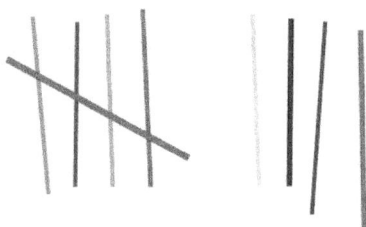

(9 lines . . .)

for those who are challenged

an anthology of Poetry inspired by . . .

Poetry Dancer

a

Poetically
Spoken
Anthology
volume I

Collector's Edition

and there is much, much more !

visit . . .

http://www.innerchildpress.com
/anthologies-sales-special.php

Also check out our Authors and
all the wonderful Books
Available at :

http://www.innerchildpress.com
/the-book-store.php

Tee Shirts

4

Sale

The Year of the Poet

$ 20.00

Small * Med. * Large * XL * XXL

http://www.innerchildpress.com/the-year-of-the-poet.php

Now Open for Submissions

World Healing World Peace

support it

www.worldhealingworldpeacepoetry.com

go to Web Site for Submission Guidelines

www.worldhealingworldpeacepoetry.com

This Anthological Publication
is underwritten solely by

Inner Child Press

Inner Child Press is a Publishing Company Founded and Operated by Writers. Our personal publishing experiences provides us an intimate understanding of the sometimes daunting challenges Writers, New and Seasoned may face in the Business of Publishing and Marketing their Creative "Written Work".

For more Information

Inner Child Press

www.innerchildpress.com

~ *fini* ~

www.ingramcontent.com/pod-product-compliance
Lightning Source LLC
LaVergne TN
LVHW051052080426
835508LV00019B/1836